Essentials of
Limited Liability Companies

Steven M. Bragg

AccountingTools®

Published by AccountingTools, Inc., Centennial, Colorado.

ISBN 978-1-64221-290-7

For more information about AccountingTools® products, visit our Web site at www.accountingtools.com.

Table of Contents

About the Author

Steven Bragg, CPA, has been the chief financial officer or controller of four companies, as well as a consulting manager at Ernst & Young. He received a master's degree in finance from Bentley College, an MBA from Babson College, and a Bachelor's degree in Economics from the University of Maine. He has been a two-time president of the Colorado Mountain Club, and is an avid alpine skier, mountain biker, and certified master diver. Mr. Bragg resides in Centennial, Colorado. He has written more than 300 books and courses, including *New Controller Guidebook*, *GAAP Guidebook*, and *Payroll Management*. He has also written *The Auditors* science fiction trilogy.

Steven maintains the accountingtools.com web site, which contains continuing professional education courses, the Accounting Best Practices podcast, and thousands of articles on accounting subjects.

Buy Additional AccountingTools Courses

AccountingTools offers more than 1,500 hours of CPE courses, with concentrations in accounting, auditing, finance, taxation, and ethics. Related courses that you might like include:

- C Corporation Tax Guide
- Partnership Tax Guide
- S Corporation Tax Guide
- Types of Business Entities

Go to accountingtools.com/cpe to view these additional courses.

AccountingTools®

Essentials of Limited Liability Companies

Introduction

A limited liability company (LLC) is a business entity that provides its owners with the limited liability protection of a corporation, while allowing earnings to pass through to the owners for tax purposes. It can also be characterized as an unincorporated association that requires much less paperwork than a corporation. In essence, an LLC combines the best features of a corporation and a partnership while not being classified as either one. An LLC is created by state statute, and is taxable as a partnership under federal tax law. We address the various aspects of an LLC in the following pages, including its advantages and disadvantages, its capital structure, and how its use impacts the payment of income taxes.

Where You Can Use the LLC Structure

The LLC structure is allowed by all 50 states, as well as the District of Columbia. Consequently, it is a valid business structure anywhere within the United States. However, LLCs are regulated at the state level, and state laws concerning how they can be operated are not always the same. There has been an effort to standardize these laws through the promulgation of a model LLC act, but many state governments have chosen to implement only portions of this baseline text. Consequently, you will need to read a summary of the LLC statute for the state in which you plan to create an LLC, to ascertain the requirements for setting up and operating it.

Which Entities Can Own an LLC

The investors in an LLC are not limited to individuals. It is also possible for non-United States citizens and residents to be the owners of one, as can other corporations, partnerships, trusts, and LLCs. This varies from a rival organizational structure, the S corporation, for which ownership is more tightly defined.

Advantages of a Limited Liability Company

There are several advantages to the LLC structure. First, it shields the personal assets of its owners from the LLC's creditors and lenders. For example, if an LLC of which you are an owner loses a lawsuit and is forced to pay the plaintiff $1,000,000, the money can only be extracted from the assets of the LLC. Similarly, if your LLC goes bankrupt due to a lack of cash, the firm's creditors can only access its assets to settle their outstanding claims. In both cases, your personal assets cannot be accessed. Further, it could make sense to convert a sole proprietorship or a partnership structure into an LLC, to afford the owners greater protection from liability. This is an especially important option for sole proprietors, who can switch to a single-member LLC.

Note: When creditors know that a business is structured as an LLC, they may be more inclined to negotiate over the settlement terms for outstanding obligations, since they know they cannot pursue the personal assets of the firm's members.

A second advantage is that the LLC owners (known as members) can enter into an agreement that specifies how taxable income and losses are to be allocated among the members. This approach differs from an S corporation, where allocations are strictly on a per-share basis. It is also useful when there is an expectation that the firm will generate losses over the near term. In this situation, the losses are passed through to the owners, which they can deduct against their other income, thereby minimizing their income taxes.

A third advantage is when a business is at risk of significant lawsuits. When this is the case, it may be too expensive to obtain comprehensive insurance coverage (since insurers will need high premiums to offset the expected payouts). In this situation, an LLC can be used to limit losses to just those assets held within the business; the personal assets of the owners will be beyond the reach of anyone demanding payment from the organization.

A fourth advantage is that the liabilities of an LLC are considered to be contributions of the members, which means that debt increases member basis. This does not happen in an S corporation, unless a shareholder directly lends assets to the corporation.

A fifth advantage is that the IRS allows you to choose between corporate tax treatment or passing through taxable income and losses to the LLC's members. The pass-through option is usually taken, but taxing the LLC entity instead allows you to retain more profits within the business – which can be useful when the firm is growing rapidly, and needs to fund a large amount of working capital.

A final advantage is that the LLC structure can be used for any number of members. Thus, it can have just one member, or more than 100.

Note: While an LLC can have an unlimited number of members, it typically has no more than ten. The reason is that ownership becomes more complex with more owners. When there are many owners, it becomes more advantageous to use a corporation structure, which makes it easier for shareholders to buy and sell shares in the business.

In short, the owners of many businesses should consider using the LLC structure for their firms, especially if their organizations have significant liabilities and they prefer to report business income on their personal income tax returns. To make the decision easier, creating an LLC or converting an existing business into one is generally quite easy – most state governments allow it to be done on a relatively simple form, along with a modest filing fee and an annual report fee.

EXAMPLE

Ernest wants to start a company that sells chairs for business executives with bad backs, which he will call Laid Back Corporation. He plans to invest $500,000 of his own money into the venture, which will call for the construction of a production line and the accumulation of a certain amount of inventory. In reviewing the risks to which the business might be subjected, he realizes that customers could sue the business on the grounds that it has worsened their back conditions, and try to collect on medical bills for remedial procedures. Even one of these lawsuits could bankrupt the company and wipe out his own assets. To eliminate the risk of these lawsuits impacting his personal assets, he decides to structure the company as an LLC, so that creditors can only access the assets of the business.

Disadvantages of a Limited Liability Company

There are a few disadvantages to the LLC structure. First, it is not allowed in some states for certain purposes, such as the provision of professional services[1], banking, or insurance. Or, a state may impose certain requirements on the members when professional services are being offered, such as not being able to exempt themselves from liability for their own malpractice. Also, some states require that licensed professionals obtain a certifying statement from their licensing board, stating that their certifications are current. Furthermore, these professionals may be required to obtain malpractice insurance.

> **Tip:** Contact the LLC filing office in the state in which you want to set up an LLC. If that office does not allow you to set up an LLC for your line of work, then there is no need to proceed with the other details in this manual – you simply cannot set up the LLC.

> **Note:** In some states, professionals are not allowed to form an LLC. For these people, an alternative is the limited liability partnership (LLP). It is intended for a professional practice in which the partners want to avoid personal liability. In this arrangement, each partner is still individually liable for his or her own malpractice, but is shielded from malpractice claims against their partners in the organization.

A second disadvantage is that owners are forced to keep separate records of their personal and business assets, so there is no intermingling of assets. This separation is needed to ensure that creditors cannot access any of the owners' personal property. This might be too much bother for people who are running small businesses on the side, such as someone operating a consulting business out of a spare room in his house on weekends.

A third disadvantage is that the ownership of an LLC is not in the form of stock certificates. This can be a concern when the owners want to offer stock options to their

---

[1] Examples of professional services are attorneys, doctors, physical therapists, psychologists, social workers, marriage and family therapists, and professional counselors.

employees, or sell shares to venture capital firms. In these cases, it would make more sense to form a corporation, where shares in the business are issued to the owners in the form of stock certificates. And, because there are no shares in an LLC, it is impossible to issue different classes of ownership to investors, as would be the case when a corporation issues common stock and several types of preferred stock to investors.

> **Note:** Though we have just noted the benefits of forming a corporation, rather than an LLC, a corporation is more difficult to maintain, with requirements for board meetings, shareholder meetings, meeting minutes, tax filings, and so forth.

EXAMPLE

Felipe works for an auditing firm during the day, and provides services as a controls analyst for local companies on the weekends. He needs essentially no assets for the controls analysis work, has no investment in it, and sees minimal risk arising from his analysis activities. Accordingly, he decides to operate the side business as a sole proprietorship, rather than an LLC.

The Economic Entity Principle

An especially valuable aspect of an LLC is that it shields the owners from any liabilities incurred by the business. However, for the limited liability benefit to take effect, the owners must follow the *economic entity principle*. This principle states that the recorded activities of a business entity should be kept separate from the recorded activities of its owners. This means that you must maintain separate accounting records and bank accounts for the business, and not intermix them with the assets and liabilities of its owners. Also, you must specifically associate every business transaction with that business.

> **Tip:** Always document your business transactions and major LLC decisions. Otherwise, a court might rule that a poorly-documented LLC does not actually exist, and hold its owners personally liable for the debts of the business.

The economic entity principle is a particular concern when a business is just being started, for that is when the owners are most likely to commingle their funds with those of the business. A typical outcome is that a trained accountant must be brought in after the entity begins to grow, in order to sort through earlier transactions and remove those that should be more appropriately linked to the owners.

> **Tip:** Be extremely careful about offering personal guarantees for debts incurred by the business, since these guarantees will allow creditors to access your personal assets to pay off liabilities incurred by the business – even if it is structured as an LLC.

The Capital Structure of an LLC

There is a substantial amount of ownership flexibility associated with an LLC. Any investor can make a financial contribution to an LLC, which may be in the form of cash, property, services, or even a promise to contribute one or more of these items to the business at some point in the future. In exchange, each party receives a percentage ownership share in the firm's assets, which is called a *capital interest*. This capital interest is assigned in the form of a number of membership units, which are similar to the shares issued by a corporation. For example, a member who owns one-quarter of an LLC might own 250 out of 1,000 membership units. Or, the membership interest might simply be stated as a 25% capital interest in the entity. In either case, this ownership interest is used to assign assets to the members in the event of a sale or dissolution of the LLC. This interest is also used to pay any members who want to sell their interests back to the other members. In addition, and depending on the operating agreement, this membership interest can be used to apportion the LLC's profits and losses to its members. Alternatively, the operating agreement can specify that profits and losses be apportioned in some other way that does not reflect the underlying ownership interests. This distribution of profits and losses, however it may be devised, is based on the distributive share of profits and losses stated in the operating agreement. A *distributive share* is the amount that is allocated to each member each year for tax purposes. All members are taxed on their distributive shares, even if they did not receive a distribution from the LLC. In most cases, the capital interest in an LLC matches the distributive share accorded to each member.

EXAMPLE

Susie, George, and Evan decide to found an LLC, All Seasons Cards, LLC. Susie and George each contribute $150,000, while Evan contributes property worth $150,000, resulting in each person having a one-third share in the business. Under the entity's ownership agreement, each member is allocated one-third of any profits or losses that will be generated by the business. Further, if any of them decides to sell out to the remaining two members, he or she will receive one-third of the current value of the LLC.

EXAMPLE

David and Shannon decide to form an LLC, with David contributing $100,000 and Shannon contributing her labor for a 50% interest in the entity. However, the operating agreement states that David will receive 60% of the profits for the first two years, to reflect his up-front payment, while Shannon will receive 40% during that period. After two years, the pair will split all profits and losses equally.

The IRS states that special allocations of profits or losses to certain members that exceeds the percentage of their ownership interest are only valid when they have a substantial economic impact. This means that such allocations cannot be designed just to assist a member in avoiding income taxes. For example, an oversized distributive share would not be allowed when the intent was clearly to distribute a large business loss to the member most in need of a large loss to offset her taxable gains from other activities.

> **Tip:** An LLC's operating agreement should clearly state how member interests in the business are valued, which reduces any conflict over how much each party will receive if they were to leave the business. In addition, the operating agreement should state how this payment will be made, such as in a lump sum, or perhaps in a series of installment payments.

In the accounting for an LLC, each member should have a separate capital account. These account balances are used as the basis for distributions to members if the entity is sold or liquidated. Thus, if Anna's capital account balance is $100,000 and Betty's is $50,000, then the sale of their LLC for $300,000 should result in $200,000 of the proceeds being apportioned to Anna, and $100,000 to Betty.

There may be cases in which a member has a negative capital account balance. This can happen when losses have been allocated to a member that exceeds her account balance, or perhaps when member distributions are greater than their capital account balance. This can be an important issue when an LLC is sold or liquidated, or when a member interest is sold, because these negative balances must be restored to a zero balance. This can be done by requiring such members to pay more cash or property into the LLC to bring their balances to zero. However, requiring the replenishment of a capital account balance essentially means that the limited liability benefit of having an LLC is being breached (since members are promising to personally pay for LLC deficits), so many LLC operating agreements do not require a negative balance replenishment.

Impact of Securities Laws

For an LLC with only a few members who are all involved in the business, there is no risk of breaching the securities laws of the United States. These laws are designed to protect investors from unscrupulous business operators, and are only triggered when there are passive investors in a business. If these laws *are* triggered, then all membership interests in the firm must be registered with the Securities and Exchange Commission (SEC), as well as the equivalent state-level agency. This registration process is exceedingly time-consuming and will likely require the expenditure of significant funds on legal fees, and so is to be avoided if at all possible. There are several ways to keep an LLC from having to go through this registration process, which are as follows:

- Set up the LLC as being member-managed (see the next section), so that all members are considered to be participants in the business. This means that the members should be actively engaged in the LLC's business activities.
- Buy out inactive members. The securities laws may be interpreted quite strictly, so if any members plan to drop out of daily business activities, consider buying them out.

- See if an exemption from the securities laws applies. It may be classified as a private offering, for which ownership transfers may not be transferred. A good choice is the Regulation D exemption, as discussed next.

A good way to ensure that no securities laws are breached is to use the Regulation D exemption, which is described in the SEC's Rules 504, 505, and 506. In general, to sell ownership interests in an LLC, the firm must only sell ownership interests to accredited investors[2] and cannot contact prospective investors through a general solicitation, such as advertising or free seminars that are open to the public. If a prospective investor is interested in purchasing an ownership interest in the LLC, the firm sends them a boilerplate questionnaire to fill out, in which they state that they are accredited investors. This form provides the LLC with legal protection, in case the SEC questions whether the ownership interest is protected by Regulation D.

Membership certificates issued under Regulation D are not initially registered, which means that a restriction statement appears on the back of each certificate. This statement essentially prohibits a member from selling to a third party. A sample statement is:

> The securities represented by this certificate have been acquired for investment and have not been registered under the Securities Act of 1933. Such securities may not be sold or transferred or pledged in the absence of such registration unless the business receives an opinion of counsel reasonably acceptable to the business, stating that such sale or transfer is exempt from the registration and prospectus delivery requirements of said Act.

Tip: Registering membership interests as securities is a gray area of the law, so it makes sense to consult a securities attorney for advice before selling membership interests to passive investors.

Member Management of an LLC

The default condition when an LLC is created is for all members to be designated as its business managers, which is known as *member management*. This approach is most common in smaller organizations, where all members need to assist with running operations. Another option is for the members to pick one or more of their number to be the designated managers of the business, in which case these individuals will be stated as such in the LLC filing documents. Having a few designated managers makes more sense when outside investors have been solicited to invest funds in the business, but who are not interested in its actual operations. Having a designated manager is also a good option when the founding members do not have sufficient management expertise, and so call upon a more experienced person to run the organization for them. As noted in the last of the preceding examples, an LLC manager does not necessarily

---

[2] An accredited investor is an individual who earns more than a minimum income threshold per year, or who has more than a minimum net worth threshold, or is a business with assets exceeding a minimum threshold level, or which meets at least one of several other criteria.

have to also be one of its members; thus, a manager might not be an investor in the business. No matter who is chosen to be the manager of an LLC, that person is assumed to be serving in that role for an indefinite period of time, until he or she is replaced by the members.

> **Note:** The members of an LLC will not lose their personal liability protection if they decide to elevate a non-member into a manager role. This situation differs from a limited partnership, where the general partner is required by law to be personally liable for the obligations of the business.

No matter who is managing an LLC, its members still have the right to swap out managers, amend its operating agreement, approve the admission of new members, approve the transfer of an existing LLC membership to a new party, and dissolve or merge the business. When making these decisions, member voting rights are typically based on the size of their ownership interests in the LLC, though this can vary by state, and is subject to the existence of any voting allocations set forth in the operating agreement.

When an LLC is organized as member managed, any of the members can legally commit the LLC to a contract, since each of these people is considered to be an agent of the entity. When the LLC is organized as being managed by a specific subset of members, then only those members can commit the LLC to a contract. In the latter case, this usually means that non-participating members are not considered to be agents of the business. Further, an LLC will usually not be forced to adhere to the terms of a contract to which one of its members committed the organization, if the requirements of the contract are clearly beyond the normal range of the firm's business activities.

> **Tip:** If you are uncomfortable having another member commit your LLC to business arrangements, it might make more sense to form an LLC in which you are the sole member. In short, if you are contemplating going into business with a person who has a reputation for being a spendthrift, don't do it.

Routine, ongoing business decisions within an LLC do not require formal member meetings, nor do they call for member votes or written consent forms. Nonetheless, certain decisions, as previously noted, do require the consent of the members. If so, the firm's operating agreement should state the rules under which member meetings will be held, noting who can call them, how much notice should be given, what constitutes a quorum, and so forth.

There are also non-ordinary business events where it might be prudent to call a member meeting. For example, the members might want to ratify a decision to make a large investment, or to sell off a major product line. Or, perhaps one of the members has an ownership interest in another firm that the LLC might buy, and this issue should be discussed before a buyout offer is made. The exact circumstances calling for a member meeting will depend on the circumstances.

> **Tip:** If an LLC has non-participating members, it can make sense to hold a year-end meeting for them, so that they can be brought up to speed on what is happening within the organization. This is not a statutory requirement, but can assist with member relations.

Start-Up Capital Tax Issues

As just noted, someone can become an investor in an LLC by contributing cash, property, services, or the promise of a future contribution to it. There are specific tax implications associated with each of these options, which are described in this section.

When you invest cash in an LLC, your initial tax basis is the amount of cash paid in. This basis will change over time, as your share of the firm's profits and losses are added to or subtracted from the initial basis. When you eventually sell your interest in the LLC, the amount of taxable income generated will be the amount received, minus the tax basis at that time.

EXAMPLE

David makes an initial cash investment of $200,000 in Dual Therapeutics LLC. He sells his ownership interest in the company two years later, for $280,000. The $200,000 is his tax basis, which is subtracted from the sale price to arrive at taxable income on the transaction of $80,000.

The situation is somewhat different when an investment is made in the form of property. For example, an investor could contribute real estate, a delivery van, or a patent to an LLC in exchange for an ownership interest. If this property has appreciated in value (as is especially common with real estate) since the investor initially acquired it, the transfer to the LLC is usually tax-free. However, the contributing investor will have to pay income tax on the amount of this appreciation when his or her interest in the business is eventually sold. This means that any tax due on the property appreciation is merely being deferred until a gain is eventually realized from the sale of the individual's membership interest.

EXAMPLE

Adam owns a warehouse that he acquired ten years ago for $300,000, and which is now worth $500,000. He transfers the building into a new LLC that will store imported furniture in the warehouse. Adam's stake in the LLC is worth $500,000, which is the value of his investment in it. A year later, Adam sells his ownership interest for $550,000. The gain on which he must pay income tax is $250,000, which is the sale price of $550,000 minus his original acquisition price (i.e., tax basis) of $300,000.

> **Tip:** Depending on the situation, an investor who contributes property to an LLC might have to pay tax on its appreciated value if the LLC later sells the asset, or if the LLC distributes profits back to the investor within a few years of the property contribution.

A particular concern is when an investor contributes property to a multi-member LLC that has a mortgage attached to it. Because LLC members share debts with each other, the amount of this mortgage is allocated among all the members in proportion to their distributive shares. This debt allocation increases the tax basis of the membership interest of every receiving member, thereby reducing any taxable gain on which income tax might have to be paid later. Since the mortgage has been apportioned among the members, the contributing member now owes less than had been the case prior to the contribution. This reduction in debt obligation is treated for tax purposes as a cash payout to that party.

EXAMPLE

Malcolm contributes a $400,000 property to an LLC, along with an associated $100,000 mortgage. There are four members, each with a 25% distributive share. For tax purposes, $25,000 of the mortgage is considered to be part of the ownership interest of each member, so Malcolm is left with a $25,000 mortgage liability for which he is responsible; this constitutes a $75,000 gain for Malcolm, which reduces the tax basis of his ownership interest in the LLC.

What about cases in which an investor acquires an ownership interest in an LLC by providing services to it? For example, someone might be willing to work for free for 1,000 hours in exchange for 10% ownership interest. In this case, the individual must pay income taxes on the value of the interest received, as though the business had issued the person a paycheck instead.

EXAMPLE

Russell is a top-notch programmer with no cash, who wants to own a share of Nite-Time Deluxe LLC, which uses sensors to monitor the sleep patterns of babies during the night and issue alerts to their parents in the event of a problem. The other members grant Russell a 10% interest in the LLC in exchange for his production of a phone app on which the firm's technology will run. For tax purposes, this work is classified as personal services income for Russell, who will have to pay tax on it in the current year, even though he was not paid for the work.

An option for avoiding the payment of taxes on the value of services provided is to acquire a profits-only interest in the LLC, rather than a more-standard ownership interest in its assets. In this case, income taxes are only due on the individual's share of the LLC's profits (if any). The downside is that the person will not share in any profits from the eventual sale of the business.

> **Tip:** Despite the aforementioned tax problem with providing services in exchange for an ownership interest, this may still be a better approach than waiting to earn enough cash to purchase an ownership interest. The reason is that the LLC may increase in value over time, so the ownership percentage acquired at a later date for the specified amount of money may be less than would have been the case if you had made the purchase right now in exchange for services provided.

Yet another option is for an investor to borrow money and then use the cash to acquire an interest in an LLC. There is no immediate tax impact from this financing decision, since, from the perspective of the LLC, this is merely a standard cash payment for an ownership interest. How the investor came by the cash is not of concern to the LLC.

The Income Tax Pass-Through of an LLC

An LLC is similar to a sole proprietorship and a partnership, in that the profits or losses of the entity are passed through to its members. This means that the members must recognize their apportioned shares of the profits or losses within their individual tax returns. This approach centralizes the tax reporting with individual tax returns, sidestepping the need for a tax return for the entity as a whole – which is a less complex endeavor for many smaller businesses. However, it also means that the members will need substantial distributions from the LLC if they are to pay the associated income taxes. This outflow of cash from the LLC can constrain its ability to grow. Thus, the income tax pass-through is a simpler tax reporting option, but requires a cash outflow from the business.

EXAMPLE

Carol and Blair invest $25,000 and $75,000, respectively, to start an LLC. Because of the differential in the amounts invested, the firm's operating agreement states that Carol owns 25,000 membership units, while Blair owns 75,000 units. The agreement also states that profits and losses will be allocated in proportion to the number of membership units owned, so Carol will receive ¼ of the profits and losses, while Blair will receive ¾. Each person will then pay income taxes on the amount allocated to them by the LLC each year.

An advantage of this approach is that any losses passed through to the members can be deducted from their other earnings, thereby reducing their overall tax bills. This is especially common during the first few years of an LLC's existence, when it is more likely to be incurring losses before it becomes fully established.

We noted in the preceding example that profits and losses were "allocated" to the owners of an LLC. This does not necessarily mean that the allocated amounts were actually paid out to the owners. If the firm is in need of cash, its members may decide to leave the cash within the firm, while they pay taxes on the allocated profits out of their own pockets. This is an especially common situation during the early years of a business, when it is still struggling to generate profits. Some states do not want excessive distributions from an LLC to bankrupt it, and so require that distributions can only be made when the entity will still be solvent and able to pay its bills after the distributions are made.

> **Tip:** Do not distribute such large amounts to members that the firm is effectively breaching statutory requirements to keep the firm solvent, or else the courts can find that the members are liable to the firm's creditors for the excess amount of the distributions.

An alternative is for the LLC to take an election to be taxed as a normal corporation. While the related tax filings are increased, this approach is more likely to leave cash within the business, which can assist it in growing. Also, this approach is tax-beneficial when the tax rates of an LLC's owners are higher than the federal tax rate for corporations, which currently stands at 21%.

Member Compensation Within an LLC

The members of an LLC generally do not pay themselves a salary. Instead, they jointly decide upon how much cash can be distributed to the members, which is then issued based on the distributive share of each member. However, any member working within an LLC can also choose to receive a salary; this is a more common arrangement when just one member is acting as the managing member and is paid a salary for that service, while the other members are not directly involved in the business. This managing member may insist on being paid a salary, in order to avoid the vagaries of LLC profits that may bounce around over time.

In cases where a salary is paid to a member, the LLC records these payments as a business expense, which it can subtract from its revenues in order to arrive at a net profit figure. This salary expense will reduce the amount of profit that can then be distributed to the members.

LLC Tax Filings

If the single owner of an LLC has elected to take pass-through profits and losses from the entity for tax reporting purposes (which is the default situation), then the LLC entity does not need to file any tax returns. Instead, the owner files his or her normal Form 1040, along with Schedule C, *Profit or Loss from Business (Sole Proprietorship),* on which is listed the person's share of any allocated profits or losses from the business. In addition, a Form SE, *Self-Employment Tax*, must be filed. The Form SE is used to report the amount of social security and Medicare tax that the individual owes on any allocated profits. Any member-manager of an LLC will have to pay self-employment taxes on any profits distributed to him or her, which is not the case for inactive owners.

Tip: A member-manager of an LLC might consider converting the entity into an S corporation, since no self-employment tax is imposed on the member-manager of an S corporation for any earnings allocated to that person. This issue only impacts the member-manager, since self-employment taxes are not imposed on earnings allocated to inactive owners.

EXAMPLE

Aaron is the sole owner of an LLC, which has four employees who are paid wages. For the purpose of paying employment taxes, the LLC is considered to be separate from Aaron. The LLC is liable for payroll taxes on the wages paid to its four employees. In addition, the LLC must file employment tax returns, make employment tax deposits, and provide year-end payroll tax summaries to its employees. In addition, Aaron is subject to self-employment tax on his net earnings from self-employment with respect to the LLC's operations. Aaron is not an employee of the LLC for payroll tax purposes. Instead, he must report the LLC's income and expenses on his Schedule C, and calculate his self-employment tax on Schedule SE.

If an LLC has two or more owners, then the entity must file a Form 1065, *U.S. Return of Partnership Income*, which is an informational return[3]. This can be a relatively complicated tax return, since it must include the capital contributions from and distributions to each member, as well as any allocations and distributions of profits. The LLC must also issue a Schedule K-1, *Partner's Share of Income, Deductions, Credits, Etc.*, to each member. The K-1 itemizes the profits, losses, credits, and deductions that have been allocated to each member, which the recipient then uses to prepare his or her own Form 1040 individual tax return.

If the LLC is expected to earn a profit for its full fiscal year, then its members are expected to make quarterly estimated tax payments to the IRS over the course of that year. The IRS will charge interest and penalties if this is not done. This may require quarterly distributions from the LLC to the members, so that they will have sufficient cash to make these payments.

If the owners of an LLC elect to take corporate tax treatment instead of the pass-through approach, then the tax filing situation is different. Under the corporate tax filing approach, the members are paid salaries through the entity, and do not have profits and losses pass through to them; instead, the LLC pays income taxes. To take this election, the LLC files Form 8832, *Entity Classification Election*, on which it elects to be classified as an association taxable as a corporation. This election will continue until such time as the members choose to switch back to using the more common pass-through approach (which can only be changed at a minimum of every five years, with few exceptions). The firm will then have to file a corporate tax return on Form 1120, *U.S. Corporation Income Tax Return*.

---

[3] An LLC with at least two members is classified as a partnership for federal income tax purposes. An LLC with just one member is not considered to be separate from its owner for income tax reporting purposes (as stated in IRS Form 3402).

> **Note:** Filing a Form 8832 does not convert an LLC into a corporation. The firm will still be an LLC in all other respects; it simply changes how it deals with income taxes.

The conversion of an LLC to corporate tax treatment involves the consideration of a few issues, so be aware of them before making the switch. It will involve having the LLC pay the payroll taxes of any members receiving a salary through the entity. Also, it is usually only a cost-effective approach when the business is solidly profitable and there is an expectation of it remaining in that condition for at least the next five years (which is when the members can switch back to pass-through reporting). Further, the LLC will now have to make quarterly estimated income tax payments to the IRS, rather than its members.

An LLC is also subject to the tax burdens imposed on other business organizational structures, such as state income taxes (if applicable) and franchise taxes. A *franchise tax* is a privilege tax imposed on any taxable entity formed or organized within a state or doing business in it. The amount paid is generally small, though California's tax is relatively substantial (currently $800 per year). In addition, an LLC must pay employment taxes on its non-member staff, and withhold income taxes from both these staff and any guaranteed payments made to its members.

The Limited Liability of an LLC

As already stated, an LLC provides its members with limited liability protection, so that only the assets within the entity are subject to creditor claims. However, creditors can access the personal assets of members in the following situations:

- When a member personally guarantees the loans of the LLC. In this case, the lender can access personal assets if the assets of the LLC are not sufficient to settle its claims.
- When a member personally engages in a negligent act, such as running into a pedestrian while driving a car owned by the LLC. In this case, the injured pedestrian can pursue either the member or the LLC (if the accident occurred while engaged in company business). This type of liability can be offset by adequate liability insurance coverage.
- When a member breaches his or her duty of care to the LLC, where they do not operate it in the best interests of the entity and its members. If any damages result from this breach, the member causing it can be held personally liable. This situation usually only arises when a member engages in fraudulent or illegal behavior that clearly damages the business. It is not an issue when a member simply makes poor business decisions.
- When an LLC pays out funds to its members that the entity cannot afford. If the LLC is sued by a third party for lack of payment, the member who approved the payout can be personally liable for the distribution.

Tip: If an LLC is organized to provided professional services (such as accounting, tax advice, or health care), then state law will likely make each professional working within it personally liable for his or her own acts of malpractice. Malpractice insurance can be purchased to mitigate this risk.

EXAMPLE

Kelly, Ryan, and Tatiana have just formed an LLC, with equal contributions to it from each of the new members. They want to invest in business real estate on the south side of town, where business prospects are somewhat questionable, but property prices are affordable. Kelly and Tatiana research the proposed area, finding that the crime rate is higher, city services are lower, and foot traffic is minimal. They disclose this information to Ryan, who is against the idea of making a purchase. Kelly and Tatiana override his veto and purchase property in the targeted area. It turns out to be a disastrous investment. However, Ryan cannot successfully sue Kelly and Tatiana for making a bad business decision, because they fully disclosed to him all of the information they used to make the purchase decision.

However, if Tatiana had supported the purchase decision because she already secretly owned the targeted property and would benefit from selling it to the LLC, then she would be personally liable if she were sued for a breach of her duty of care to the LLC.

It is possible for the limited liability feature of an LLC to be stripped away, thereby exposing its members to the organization's liabilities. This can occur when a court finds that the organization was not operated as a separate business entity. This typically occurs only in the most unusual circumstances, where the members are clearly operating the LLC as a direct extension of their personal activities. To keep this from happening, be sure to maintain a separate set of accounting records and bank accounts for the entity, so that the personal financial arrangements of its members are kept separate. Also, maintain a sufficient amount of funds in the business to ensure that it can settle its obligations in a timely manner. Otherwise, a court might rule that the organization was set up as a sham enterprise, with the intent to defraud creditors and lenders. Finally, avoid all transactions that even hint of being fraudulent. If fraud can be proven against the entity or its members, then the firm's limited liability protection may be stripped away.

Tip: A single-entry bookkeeping system (such as a check book) can be sufficient for a smaller LLC, and is usually considered an adequate recordkeeping system. However, a business of any size should use a double-entry system, so that a proper set of financial statements (including a balance sheet) can be constructed for it.

A further concern is whether the creditors of a member can pursue the assets of an LLC of which that member is an owner. Depending on the state, it may be possible for a creditor to take over a member's ownership interest in an LLC. This is essentially a lien against the ownership interest, and allows the creditor to take any profit distributions from the LLC to the member, until the underlying debt has been discharged.

In a small number of states, a creditor can petition a court to liquidate an LLC, so that the creditor can gain access to its residual assets.

The Organization of an LLC

An LLC may be managed either by its members or someone assigned to the management role. Usually, a smaller LLC is managed by its members, since they cannot afford to hire anyone to perform this task. A more profitable and larger LLC may have a separate group of hired managers. Hired managers may also make sense when the members are only interested in investing, rather than managing. Or, a member gives family members a management role, so that they can take over his or her ownership interest once they are familiar with its operations.

> **Note:** In many states, the organization of an LLC must be stated in its articles of incorporation or operating agreement, identifying who will manage it.

If certain types of management decisions are required to be stated in an operating agreement, they are likely to include only a few key decisions, such as when the entity should take on new debt, admit new members, sell major assets, dissolve the entity, and buy out an existing member.

The LLC Operating Agreement

Every LLC should have an operating agreement, covering the essential organizational transactions of the business. An *operating agreement* outlines the rules pertaining to how an organization's financial and functional decisions will be handled. Once the document is signed by the LLC's members, it acts as an official contract, binding them to its terms. At a minimum, these transactions should include the following:

- How much of the LLC's profits shall be distributed each year
- How the LLC will be managed
- How the profits and losses of the LLC will be allocated among the members
- How to buy out a member's interest in the LLC
- How to change ownership proportions when additional investments are made
- How voting power is allocated among the members
- The decisions that require member votes
- The rules under which the LLC will conduct meetings and take votes
- The situations that will trigger the dissolution of the LLC
- What the tax year and accounting method of the LLC shall be
- Whether any members will be compensated by the LLC for services rendered to it
- Whether members can sell their ownership interests to outside parties
- Whether members will be allowed to work concurrently for competing businesses
- Who owns the LLC, and in what proportions

If there is no operating agreement for an LLC, then the statutes pertaining to LLCs in the state in which it was formed will dictate how disputes are to be resolved. This can be a problem; for example, these statutes generally state that the profits and losses of an LLC be divided equally among its members, irrespective of how much they contributed to it. Consequently, if you wish to operate an LLC in a manner that differs from state statutes, having an operating agreement is essential.

In a few cases, your state's LLC laws may override the terms of your operating agreement. This usually involves a requirement that at least a majority of an LLC's members must approve amendments to the operating agreement, transfers of ownership, and the admission of new members.

Tip: Review your state-level LLC statute to determine the requirements for an LLC's operating agreement. This information can be used to develop the agreement. Preferably, have an attorney who is knowledgeable in your local LLC statute handle this task.

Essential Steps for Forming an LLC

There are a few basic steps required to form and maintain an LLC. They are as follows:

1. File articles of incorporation with your state's secretary of state office. Depending on the state, it may be called a "certificate of organization." In most states, this filing can be done online, stating the name and address of the LLC, the names of its initial members, its registered agent[4], and where to send legal notifications. If a management team will run the LLC, their names may need to be listed on the form.

Tip: Check in advance with your secretary of state's office to see if your proposed LLC business name is already being used. If so, your filing will be rejected. Also, avoid a name that is too close to another firm's name or trademark. Trademarks can be researched at www.uspto.gov.

---

2. Create an LLC operating agreement.
3. Create a binder in which to store LLC documents.
4. Hold an organizational meeting to formally adopt the operating agreement and elect officers. File the minutes of this meeting in the LLC binder.
5. Apply to the Internal Revenue Service for a tax identification number for the business.
6. Open a bank account in the name of the LLC.
7. Obtain a liability insurance policy for the LLC.

---

[4] A registered agent is a known contact for your business, who resides in the state in which the LLC is registered. A registered agent can be an individual or an entity (such as an estate or trust). An LLC can serve as its own registered agent. This definition can vary by state.

8. File an annual report for the LLC with your state's secretary of state.
9. File all required tax returns with the state and federal governments.

In addition, be sure to sign all contracts and loan agreements (essentially anything establishing an obligation for the LLC) in the name of the LLC. Otherwise, an argument can be made that you personally signed off on these contracts, making you personally liable for them. An example of a contract signature on behalf of an LLC would be:

Fireball Flight Services, LLC

By: *David King*
     David King, Member

Converting to an LLC

It is quite common for the owners of a partnership or a sole proprietorship to convert it into an LLC, usually so that they can limit their personal liabilities related to the business. If so, most state governments provide an easy conversion process, where the assets and liabilities of the existing business are shifted directly into the new one. In addition, the ownership interests of the owners are carried forward in the same proportions used for the old business. This is considered a change in legal structure, rather than a sale of the business, so there is no taxable event.

EXAMPLE

Andrew, Scott, Philip, and Ken convert their 25-25-25-25 partnership into an LLC. The operating agreement for the new entity provides each of them with a 25% capital interest in the business, along with a 25% distributive share of its profits and losses.

> **Note:** In cases where you want to convert an existing partnership into an LLC, the secretary of state's office may also require you to fill out a certificate of conversion.

If you are converting an existing organization into an LLC, there are a number of additional steps to be completed, including the following:

- Notify the Internal Revenue Service
- Notify your state's taxation department
- Notify any other government entity with which you have submitted filings in the past
- Transfer all business permits to the new entity name and federal employer identification number, such as your business license, professional license, and sales tax permit

It may also be necessary to contact your suppliers to notify them of the change, since your existing contracts with them were under the name of the prior business. If your prior business had any loans outstanding, the lender will need to be notified of the change.

In some states, reorganizing an existing business into an LLC will trigger a bulk sales law. This law is intended to protect creditors in the event of a bulk sale of business assets outside of the normal course of business. Under these laws, you must publish a notice of the conversion in the local newspaper and then wait for any creditors of the existing business to submit claims. The law's intent is to keep the owners of a business from avoiding debts by switching to a new form of organizational structure.

Business Type Comparison

The following two exhibits present a comparison of the main organizational structures that a business might use, focusing on such matters as the number of allowed owners, the income tax brackets used, and whether multiple classes of stock are allowed. The high degree of variability among these choices allows you to select a structure that most closely aligns with the needs of your business. For example:

- *Small family-owned business*. Might opt for an S corporation, due to the limited number of shareholders allowed and the protection from liability. An LLC would also be a good option.
- *Professional service provider*. Might choose a personal service corporation in order to pay lower taxes, shelter under its liability protection, and benefit from the tax deductibility of fringe benefit expenditures.
- *Rapidly growing business*. Might opt for a C corporation in order to raise money by selling shares to many shareholders.
- *Real estate investment*. Might opt to raise capital to construct a building with a limited partnership arrangement, since it protects the limited partners from creditors to some degree.

Comparison of Organizational Structures

Issue	S Corporation	C Corporation	General Partnership
Number of owners	Limited to 100 shareholders	Unlimited number of shareholders	Unlimited number of partners
Types of shareholders	Some restrictions on the types of shareholders	No restriction on the types of shareholders	No restriction on the types of partners
Income tax brackets	The brackets of the shareholders are used	A 21% income tax is imposed on the corporation	The brackets of the partners are used
Ease of formation	Subject to IRS approval	Easy	Easy, but should write a partnership agreement
Protection from creditors	Yes	Yes	No protection from creditors for the partners
Classes of stock allowed	One	Multiple	Based on percentage of ownership
Double taxation	No – income and losses pass through to shareholders	Yes – applies to any dividends paid to shareholders	No – income and losses pass through to partners
Self-employment taxes applied to owners	Only on compensation paid for services rendered; the remainder is a distribution that is free of payroll taxes	Only on compensation paid for services rendered	All distributions are subject to self-employment tax
Owners can participate in management	Yes	Yes	Yes

Comparison of Organizational Structures (continued)

Issue	Sole Proprietorship	Limited Partnership	Limited Liability Company
Number of owners	One	Must have at least one general partner and one limited partner	Unlimited number of members
Types of shareholders	Individual	No limitation on the types of partners	No restriction on the types of members
Income tax brackets	The brackets of the owner are used	The brackets of the partners are used	The brackets of the members are used
Ease of formation	Very easy, since is not a separate entity	Some difficulty, depending on the rules of the applicable state government	Relatively easy, but should write an LLC operating agreement
Protection from creditors	Not at all; the owner is liable for the obligations of the business	Only for the limited partners, who are at risk for the amount of their investments in the entity	Yes, except for cases where professional malpractice applies
Classes of stock allowed	Not applicable, since there are no shares	Not applicable, since limited partners have no voting rights	An LLC is structured so that the owners each have a membership interest in the company, not stock
Double taxation	No	No	No
Self-employment taxes applied to owners	The entity is not separable from the owner, so in effect the owner pays self-employment taxes	Only applies to the general partner	Yes, if it is a service partnership where the members cannot be classified as limited partners
Owners can participate in management	The owner is the manager	Only those classified as general partners	Yes

Summary

An LLC makes the most sense for certain clearly-defined situations. For example, it is a good choice when the number of owners is relatively small, with ten members being a reasonable maximum. Beyond that level, it may be difficult to devise an operating agreement that can foresee the multitude of issues that can arise with a large number of owners. An LLC is also a good choice when the owners want to take home the bulk of the profits generated by the entity each year. When an LLC is designed to distribute all profits to its members, they will need a large cash distribution from the business in order to pay the associated income taxes. However, when the owners are more interested in keeping a reasonable proportion of the profits inside the business, then it might be better to elect corporate income tax treatment for the firm.

Conversely, there are a few situations in which an LLC might not be the right choice. For example, when a business is quite small and has a minimal risk of incurring liabilities (such as an at-home business with no debt), then there is not much point in forming an LLC and having to deal with the associated paperwork. Also, professional service providers may find that the state in which they are located requires them to take personal responsibility for their malpractice, in which case an LLC provides them with no protection. A final situation in which an LLC might not be the best choice is when the organization will need to raise a substantial amount of cash. If so, a better choice is a corporation, where shares can be sold to investors and perhaps sold to the public through an initial public offering.

In short, the LLC format is not a perfect organizational structure for all situations. However, it represents a good blend of the features of a corporation and a partnership, while not being classified as either one. As such, it is worth considering for many types of businesses.

Glossary

A

Accredited investor. An individual who earns more than a minimum income threshold per year, or who has more than a minimum net worth threshold, or is a business with assets exceeding a minimum threshold level, or which meets at least one of several other criteria.

C

Capital interest. A percentage ownership share in an LLC's assets.

B

Distributive share. The amount of profit or loss that is allocated to each member each year for tax purposes.

E

Economic entity principle. A principle stating that the recorded activities of a business entity should be kept separate from the recorded activities of its owners.

F

Franchise tax. A privilege tax imposed on any taxable entity formed or organized within a state or doing business in it.

L

Limited liability company. A business entity that provides its owners with the limited liability protection of a corporation, while allowing earnings to pass through to the owners for tax purposes.

M

Member management. When all members of an LLC are designated as its business managers.

O

Operating agreement. A document that outlines the rules pertaining to how an organization's financial and functional decisions will be handled.

R

Registered agent. A known contact for your business, who resides in the state in which the LLC is registered.

T

Tax basis. The value of an asset that is used when determining the taxable gain or loss when the asset is sold.

Index